SMART BRAIN RIGHT BRAIN

Know Your Body

Om KIDZ
An imprint of Om Books International

First Published in 2021 by

Om Kidz | Om Books International

Corporate & Editorial Office
A-12, Sector 64, Noida 201 301
Uttar Pradesh, India
Phone: +91 120 477 4100
Email: editorial@ombooks.com
Website: www.ombooksinternational.com

Sales Office
107, Ansari Road, Darya Ganj
New Delhi 110 002, India
Phone: +91 11 4000 9000
Email: sales@ombooks.com

Author: Shweta Sinha
Editor: Kirti Pathak
Art & Design: Anshuman Pandey, Gaurav Bhandari, Harish Arya

ISBN: 978-93-5276-832-5

Printed in India

10 9 8 7 6 5 4 3 2 1

CONTENTS

1. All About Your Body

Your body is really amazing.

It breathes.

It eats.

It drinks.

It jumps.

It walks.

It thinks.

It talks.

Each part of our body is made up of cells, which are the tiniest form of life.

Your body has many parts.

A head full of hair

Eyes and nose

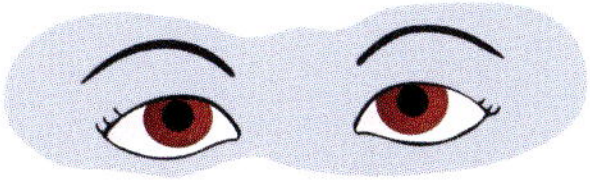

Mouth and lips

Hands and elbows

Ten little fingers

Ten little toes

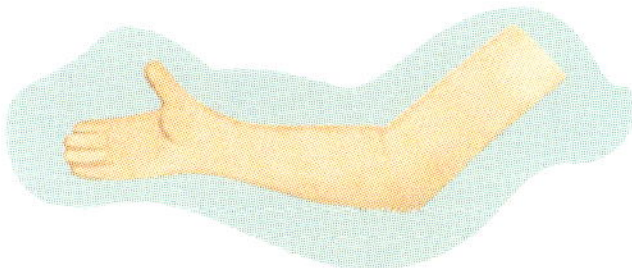

On two little feet

And all of those!

POCKET FACT

Though each of us appears different from others, inside we are all human beings.

Let's make a mini-me

You need:

- A4 size sheet
- Black marker
- Glue
- Your passport-size photo

Take a sheet of paper and draw a human shape like this.

Paste your picture as shown

Decorate your mini-me as you wish.

Draw whatever clothes you want it to wear.

Draw your favourite shoes too.

Your mini-me is ready.

POCKET FACT

The human body needs air, food and water to stay alive.

2. Head and Face

The front of your head is your **Face**.

Your face is different from everyone else's.

DID YOU KNOW?

No one looks exactly like you, unless you have an identical twin.

Your face has two **Eyes** to help you see.

It has a **Nose** to breathe and smell.

It has a **Mouth** to smile and laugh.

Your face has two little **Ears** to help you hear when your mommy calls.

Your mouth has **Lips**, **Teeth** and **Tongue**.

You chew food with your teeth.

Your tongue helps you taste.

Lips help you smile.

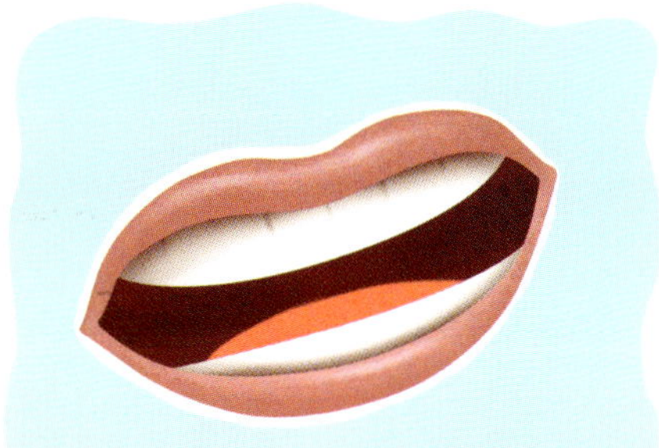

Teeth

Tongue

Lips

POCKET FACT

Always brush your teeth in the morning and at night to keep them clean and free from cavities.

The top and back of your head is covered with **Hair**. Your hair protects your head.

What colour is your hair?

Is it the same colour as your friend's?

POCKET FACT

People's hair can be black, brown, red, blonde, grey or white in colour.

3. Who's in Control?

Inside your head is your **Brain**.

Your brain is amazing.

It controls every move you make.

It thinks.

It lets you learn new things.

It even works while you sleep.

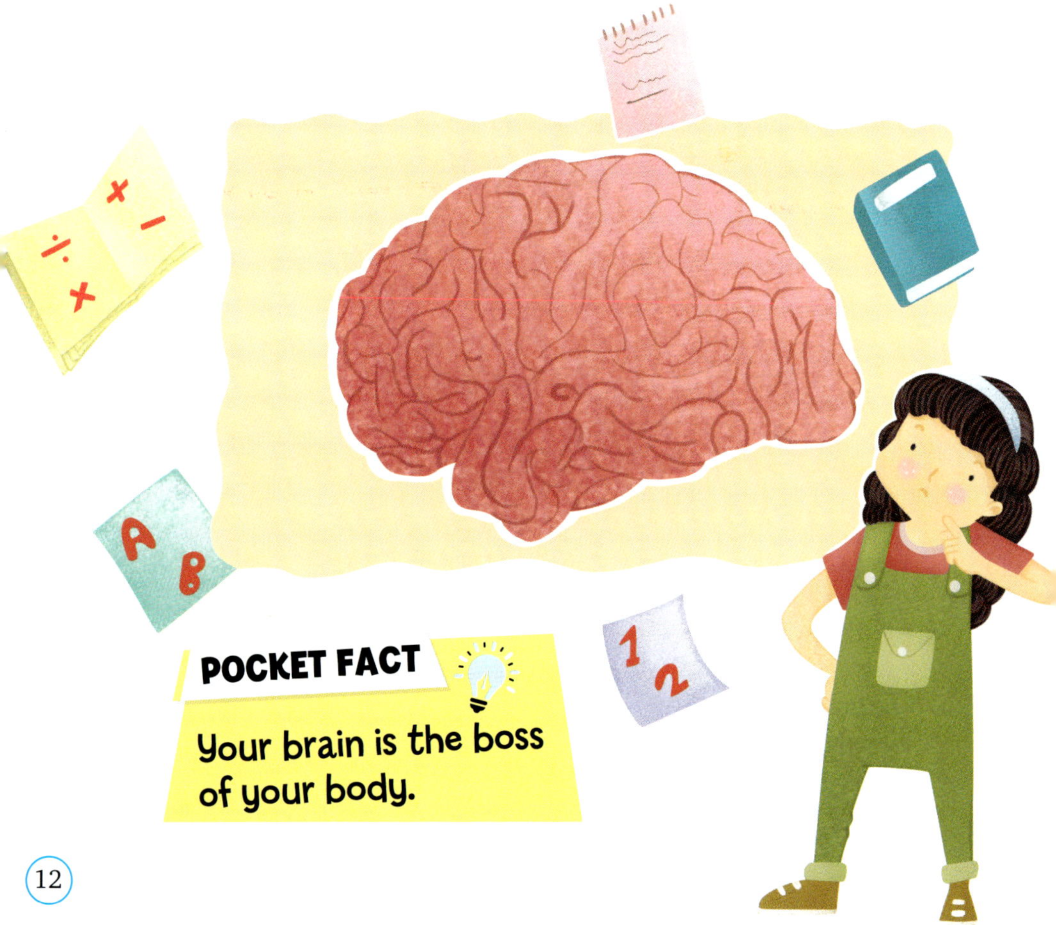

POCKET FACT

Your brain is the boss of your body.

Be good to your brain.

DID YOU KNOW?

Your brain looks like a ball of wrinkled, gray tissue.

Your brain needs exercise too.

Read, write, practise math and solve puzzles to exercise your brain.

Play games and sports.

Eat healthy food.

Wear a helmet when riding a bike to protect your head if you fall.

2. Hands and Legs

Can you count your **Hands**?

I have two. How many do you?

Can you show me where?

DID YOU KNOW?

Your shoulder connects your body to your arms.

Your hands have little **Fingers** on them. Can you wriggle them like me? Can you count them all? I counted ten. How many did you?

Ten fingers

POCKET FACT

All fingers have names. The short, thick one, set lower and apart from the other four is the thumb. The finger next to the thumb is the Index finger, the longest finger is the middle finger, then the ring finger and the smallest finger is called a Pinky.

Things you can do with your hands:

Clap

Hold a pencil

Play with toys

Pick up things

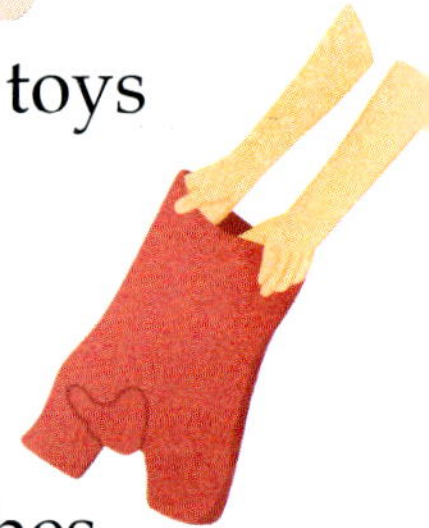

Wear clothes

Eat food

Write

You cannot hold anything without a thumb.

Touch

POCKET FACT

The hand is attached to the arm by the wrist.

What about **Legs**?

I have two. How many do you?

Can you show me your legs?

DID YOU KNOW?

Your legs are attached to your hips.

Our legs have **Feet**.

Where are your feet?

Can you show me?

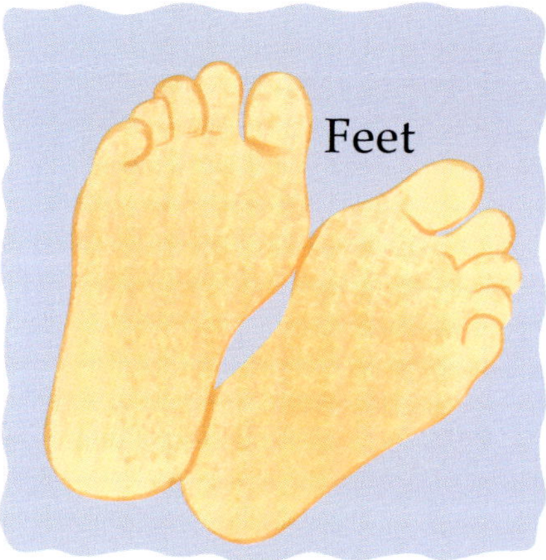

POCKET FACT

You have two feet but to play hopscotch you hop on one foot.

Your legs and feet are a great team.
They help you to

Stand

Walk

Jump

Run

Kick

Skip

Swim

POCKET FACT

More than half of the bones in your body are found in your hands and feet.

5. Skin

Your body is covered by **Skin**.

The skin protects your internal body parts.

It keeps you warm in winters and cool in summers.

POCKET FACT

Like hair, people are born with different skin colours.

6. Our Five Senses

We have five **Senses**.

We See
with our **Eyes**.

We Smell
with our **Nose**.

We Hear
with our **Ears**.

We Taste
with our **Tongue**.

We Touch
with our
Skin.

Our senses help us do all our work and also to understand the world around us.

When you see yourself in the mirror, you are using your **sense of sight**.

Your eyes help you see the pictures in a book and your mommy's smiling face.

POCKET FACT

Your eyes need light to see. That is why you cannot see in the dark.

When you smell cookies in the oven, you are using your **sense of smell**.

Your nose helps you smell the sweet scent of flowers when you are in the garden.

POCKET FACT

Your nose is connected with your mouth inside your throat.

When you hear a song, you are using your **sense of hearing**.

Your ears help you hear the dog bark, the bird sing and a baby's giggles.

POCKET FACT

Even when you close your ears, you can hear yourself breathe.

When you eat an ice-cream, you are using your **sense of taste**.

Your tongue helps you taste the milk, the yummy chocolates, and your favourite food.

POCKET FACT

The tongue has different taste buds to sense sweet, sour, salty and hot flavours.

When you touch the cool water on a hot day, you are using your **sense of touch**. You touch with your fingers.

DID YOU KNOW?

Your senses work every minute of the day.

7. Fit and Healthy

To stay fit and healthy, you need to take care of your body.

Drink lots of water.

Eat lots of fruits and vegetables.

Brush your teeth in the morning and at night.

Trim your nails.

Get plenty of sleep.

Bathe or shower every day.

Play outdoor games more.

Wash your hands before you eat.

Let's Get Active

Parts of the Face

Draw the missing parts on the face:

Label the body parts:

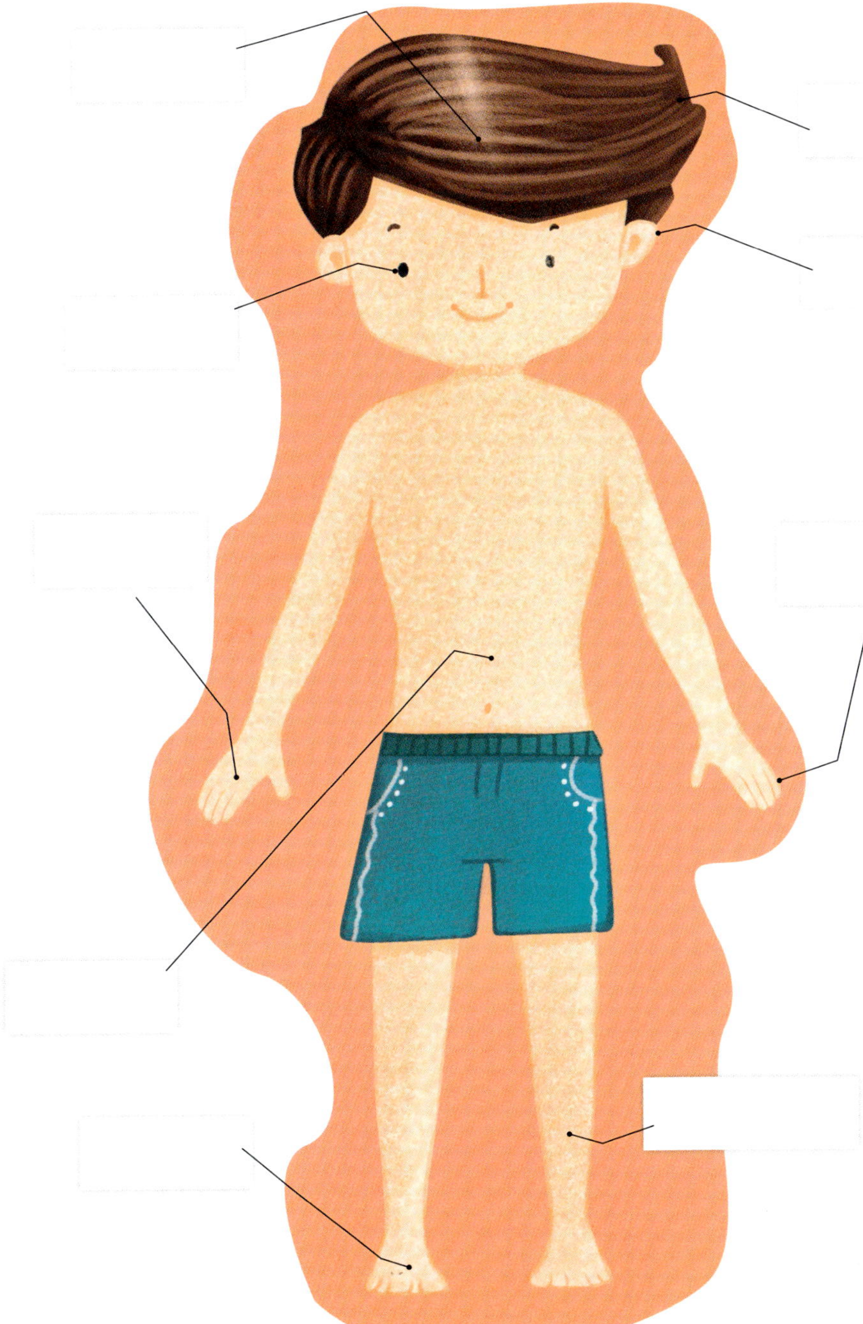

My Five Senses

Fill in the blanks:

Nose Eyes Ears Tongue Hands

1. I taste with my ____________________.
2. I see with my ____________________.
3. I smell with my ____________________.
4. I hear with my ____________________.
5. I touch with my ____________________.

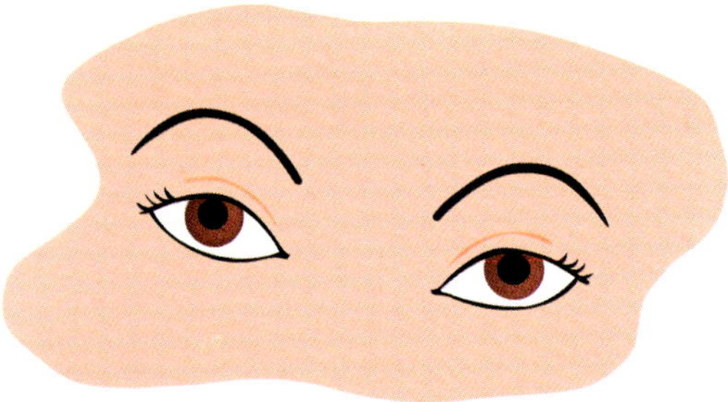

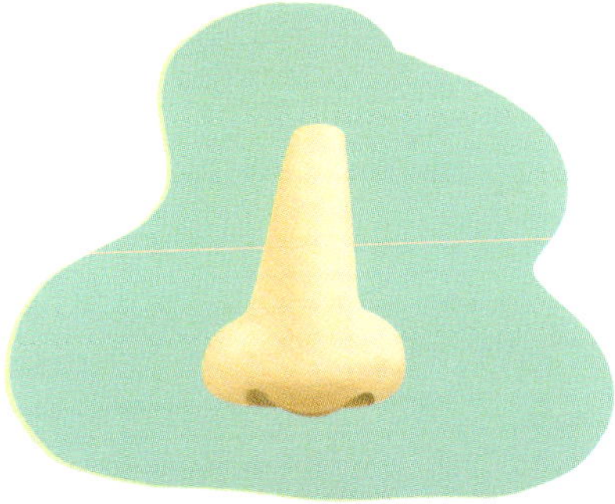

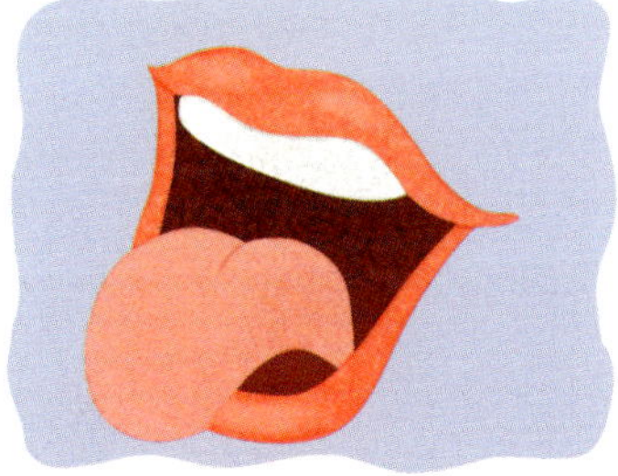

Hands or Feet?

Write 'F' for 'feet' or 'H' for hands that you would use for the following activities:

Clap loudly

Walk to school

Jump over a bump

Eat a sandwich

Stand up

Wear a T-shirt

GLOSSARY

Breathe	to take in air through the nose
Cavity	a hollow space in a tooth
Different	not alike
Hopscotch	a children's game played by hopping on onc foot
Humans	people
Identical	exactly the same
Protect	to guard from harm
Shrink	to grow smaller
Sight	to see
Twins	children born together
Wriggle	to twist or squirm

ANSWERS

Page 29.

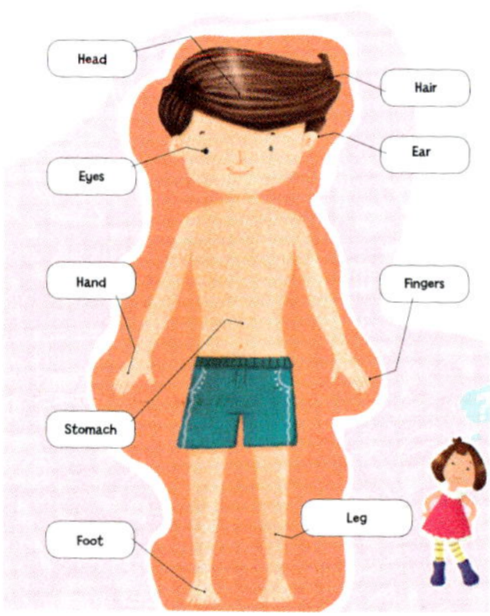

Page 30.
1. Tongue
2. Eyes
3. Nose
4. Ears
5. Hands

Page 31.

Clap loudly	H
Walk to school	F
Jump over a bump	F
Eat a sandwich	H
Stand up	F
Wear a T-shirt	H